WEST VIRGINIA REVOLUTIONARY ANCESTORS

Whose services were non-military and whose names, therefore, do not appear in Revolutionary indexes of soldiers and sailors.

Compiled by

ANNE WALLER REDDY

An Index from Manuscript Public Claims of the Revolutionary War in the Virginia State Library

CLEARFIELD

Originally published: Richmond, Virginia, 1930
Reprinted: Genealogical Publishing Co., Inc.,
Baltimore, Maryland
1963, 1973, 1979, 1983

Reprinted for
Clearfield Company, Inc. by
Genealogical Publishing Co., Inc.
Baltimore, Maryland
1995, 1996, 2001, 2003

Library of Congress Catalogue Card Number 63-3219
International Standard Book Number: 0-8063-0291-7

Made in the United States of America

TABLE OF CONTENTS

▼

FOREWORD

THIS list of names is compiled for the benefit of those who desire to trace ancestors who gave service in the Revolutionary War, but whose names do not appear in the indexes of Revolutionary soldiers and sailors.

Pacifist patriots, women as well as men, who nursed the sick and wounded, whether enemy or friend; who fed the troops; who cared for the needy families of the soldiers; who carried the dead and wounded from the battlefields.

Names in "West Virginia Revolutionary Ancestors" are taken from the Revolutionary Public Claims and are not to be found in other indexes unless both military and non-military service was rendered. Services recorded in the Public Claims are not only for supplies furnished the army and navy, but also for riding express, transporting prisoners, transporting the sick, transporting provisions, manufacturing firearms. The names of the civil officers of the county and state, serving under the new United States government, are also frequently found.

In compiling this index grateful acknowledgment is made to the Virginia State Librarian, H. R. McIlwaine, the Virginia State Archivist, Morgan P. Robinson, and his staff, Miss Stella Bass, Mrs. James Pollard and Miss Bessie Gill, without whose valuable aid and unfailing courtesy this work could not have been accomplished.

ANNE WALLER REDDY
OFFICE: 1005 East Marshall Street
Richmond, Virginia

WHAT ARE REVOLUTIONARY PUBLIC CLAIMS?

The Public Claims are the records of supplies given, and services rendered, for the purpose of carrying on the Revolutionary war.

The Act, for procuring a supply of provisions and other necessaries for the use of the Army; Virginia General Assembly, May, 1780, provides:

> Where as in the present alarming and critical situation of the war with a powerful enemy in the neighboring southern states, it may be indispensably necessary to provide and collect in proper places, with the utmost expedition, large stores of provisions, either to supply our own militia or Continental troops, or for supplying the troops sent by our good allies to the assistance of these United States; Be it enacted by the General Assembly, That the governor with the advice of council, be empowered to appoint commissioners in such counties, within the Commonwealth, as they may think necessary for the purpose of carrying this act into execution.

A Warrant is an order, or promissary note, for the money value of supplies given, or services rendered, as recorded in the Public Claims. Warrants of the Revolutionary period may be compared to the Liberty Bonds of the World War; for without the services and supplies represented by these Public Claims victory for the Continentals would have been impossible.

Under the "Commissioners of Provisions Law", commissioners were appointed in each district to collect supplies for the Revolutionary army in Virginia. Each county clerk recorded the names of those to whom warrants were issued; and in almost all instances the nature of the service is described in the warrant.

When the State of Virginia paid the Revolutionary Public Claims, the records from each county were sent to the Auditor of the State of Virginia at Richmond. There they remained inaccessible for many years, and were finally stored in the basement of the Virginia State Library.

When Dr. Earl G. Swem, now librarian at the College of William and Mary, Williamsburg, Va., was the assistant librarian of the Virginia State Library, he assembled and made available to research workers, the Revolutionary Public Claims as well as the Personal and Land Tax Books, (beginning 1782), for every county in Virginia. These papers were among the several hundred thousand pieces of manuscript material stored without order in the basement of the Library and rescued through the efforts of Dr. Swem. The value of this work done by Dr. Swem is inestimable. The Public Claims provide a record of non-military Revolutionary service to be found in no other way. The Tax Books furnish proof of land titles, dates of importance, and often supply the missing link in research work by providing information impossible to secure elsewhere.

Indexes of Revolutionary Public Claims are valuable because they contain names of patriots whose services to their country are recorded in no other place save in these manuscripts in the archives of the Virginia State Library.

WEST VIRGINIA COUNTIES—REVOLUTIONARY AND 1930 NAMES

The counties of that part of the State of Virginia, which later became West Virginia have been divided and sub-divided so many times since the days of the Revolutionary war that the following list of the Revolutionary name of a county and the names of the counties taken from it, is submitted:

REVOLUTIONARY NAME   *NAME IN 1930*

Monongalia County	Harrison County	Gilmer County
	Randolph County	Doddridge County
	Wood County	Wirt County
	Lewis County	Upshur County
	Preston County	Pleasants County
	Braxton County	Tucker County
	Barbour County	Calhoun County
	Ritchie County	Clay County
	Taylor County	Monongalia County
	Marion County	
Botetourt County	Logan County	Raleigh County
	Fayette County	Wyoming County
	Mercer County	McDowell County
Berkeley County	Jefferson County	Berkeley County
	Morgan County	
Hampshire County	Hardy County	Hampshire County
Greenbrier County	Kanawha County	Wayne County
	Monroe County	Boone County
	Mason County	Putnam County
	Cabell County	Roane County
	Nicholas County	Greenbrier County
	Jackson County	Webster County

INDEX OF NON-MILITARY REVOLUTIONARY SERVICE

In the Lands of Berkeley, Botecourt, Greenbrier, Hampshire and Monongalia Now Represented by Forty-Two Counties in West Virginia

[*Editor's Note:*—This is merely an index. It does not include the details of the service rendered by the men listed. These facts are in the Archives and may be found by a personal search; or secured from the author.]

ABBET, Benjamin..Monongalia County
Abner, John..Berkeley County
Ackins, William...Berkeley County
Adam, (.................)....................................Greenbrier County
Adams, Thomas..Berkeley County
Adamhoke, John...Berkeley County
Alderson, George..Greenbrier County
Alexander, John...Monongalia County
Alford, Robert...Greenbrier County
Algive, Manis..Hampshire County
Allan, Robert..Berkeley County
Allen, Benjamin...Berkeley County
Allen, Benjamin...Botetourt County
Allen, Robert...Berkeley County
Allen, William...Botetourt County
Aller, Peter...Berkeley County
Allimong, Jacob...Berkeley County
Allison, James..Greenbrier County
Allison, John..Greenbrier County
Allison, Joseph...Greenbrier County
Ambrous, Andrew...Berkeley County
Ambrous, Henry..Berkeley County
Anderson, Colbert.......................................Berkeley County
Anderson, John..Greenbrier County
Anderson, William.......................................Berkeley County
Anderson, William.......................................Botetourt County
Anderson, William.......................................Hampshire County
Andrew, Moses..Berkeley County

Antle, Henry ....Berkeley County
Arbuckle, John ....Greenbrier County
Arbuckle, Mathew ....Greenbrier County
Arbuckle, William ....Greenbrier County
Armentrout, Christopher ....Hampshire County
Armstrong, Robert ....Greenbrier County
Arnold, John ....Hampshire County
Ashbrook, Aaron ....Hampshire County
Ashbrook, Levi ....Hampshire County
Ashby, Benjamin ....Hampshire County
Ashby, Daniel ....Hampshire County
Ashby, Stephen ....Hampshire County
Askew, William ....Berkeley County
Athey, John ....Berkeley County
Aviss, John ....Berkeley County

BAKER, Anthony..................................Hampshire County
Baker, John...Berkeley County
Baker, Walter......................................Berkeley County
Baldwin, William.................................Berkeley County
Baldwin, William, *Senior*....................Berkeley County
Ball, *Colonel* John.............................Berkeley County
Ball, William......................................Monongalia County
Banta, Samuel.....................................Berkeley County
Barns, James.......................................Berkeley County
Barns, James.......................................Monongalia County
Barns, John...Berkeley County
Barns, Joseph, *Junior*.........................Berkeley County
Barns, Joseph, *Senior*.........................Berkeley County
Barns, William....................................Berkeley County
Barr, Philip..Berkeley County
Barrett, Edward...................................Greenbrier County
Bartholamew, Joseph............................Monongalia County
Bartlett, Mary.....................................Berkeley County
Barton, Theophilus...............................Berkeley County
Bashore, Barnard.................................Berkeley County
Bashore, George...................................Berkeley County
Bates, *Doctor*....................................Berkeley County
Batt, Thomas.......................................Berkeley County
Batten, Thomas....................................Monongalia County
Baxter, William...................................Berkeley County
Bayers, Conrad....................................Berkeley County
Baylor, *Colonel* Robert........................Berkeley County
Bealle, George.....................................Hampshire County
Beall, *Captain* Isaac...........................Berkeley County
Bear, Peter...Berkeley County
Beard, John..Berkeley County
Beard, John..Botetourt County
Beaver, Mathias...................................Hampshire County
Beaver, Michael...................................Hampshire County
Bedinger, Magdalene.............................Berkeley County
Bedinger, Peter....................................Berkeley County
Beeler, Benjamin..................................Berkeley County
Beeson, Edward...................................Berkeley County
Beeson, Henry.....................................Monongalia County
Beeson, Jacob......................................Monongalia County
Beeson, Richard...................................Berkeley County
Belestone, Thomas................................Berkeley County
Bell, Joseph..Berkeley County

Beller, Jacob	Berkeley County
Bennett, George	Berkeley County
Berry, Enoch	Hampshire County
Berry, Joel	Hampshire County
Berry, Thomas	Berkeley County
Berry, William	Hampshire County
Best, William	Greenbrier County
Bevin, Mathias	Hampshire County
Bishop, George	Berkeley County
Black, Robert	Berkeley County
Blackburn, John	Berkeley County
Blackburn, Joseph	Hampshire County
Blackburn, William	Hampshire County
Blackmore, James	Berkeley County
Blatsly, Zopher	Hampshire County
Blands, *Colonel*	Berkeley County
Blew, Uriah	Hampshire County
Blue, Abraham	Hampshire County
Blue, Garret	Hampshire County
Blue, James	Hampshire County
Blue, John	Hampshire County
Bodkin, Richard	Hampshire County
Bogard, Benjamin	Hampshire County
Bogard, Cornelius	Monongalia County
Bogard, Ezekial	Hampshire County
Boggard, Jacob	Hampshire County
Boggoss, Thomas	Berkeley County
Bogs, William	Berkeley County
Bolding, Michael	Berkeley County
Bolling, John	Berkeley County
Bond, George	Berkeley County
Booth, Caleb	Berkeley County
Booth, Daniel	Monongalia County
Booth, *Captain* James	Monongalia County
Borrichman, Michael	Berkeley County
Bourns, William	Berkeley County
Bowan, Anthony	Greenbrier County
Bower, George	Berkeley County
Bower, Henry	Berkeley County
Bowman, Thomas	Berkeley County
Boyd, John	Berkeley County
Boyd, William	Berkeley County
Boydstone, David	Monongalia County

Boydstone, George	Monongalia County
Boyle, Henry	Berkeley County
Boyle, Stephen	Berkeley County
Boyles, William	Berkeley County
Bozart, Henry	Berkeley County
Bozwell, George	Berkeley County
Brabson, John	Berkeley County
Bradford, Peter	Berkeley County
Bradshaw, Hugh	Greenbrier County
Bradshaw, James	Greenbrier County
Bradshaw, William	Greenbrier County
Brady, William	Greenbrier County
Brandenburg, Matthias	Hampshire County
Branson, Amos	Hampshire, County
Breaden, Elija	Greenbrier County
Breedg, George	Monongalia County
Brian, Christopher	Greenbrier County
Brink, Ursulia	Hampshire County
Briscoe, *Captain* George	Berkeley County
Brisco, John	Berkeley County
Britton, Jonathan	Berkeley County
Broadhead, D.	Berkeley County
Broobeck, Romanus	Berkeley County
Brooks, John	Berkeley County
Broshiers, Zepheniah	Berkeley County
Brown, Daniel	Berkeley County
Brown, James	Botetourt County
Brown, James	Hampshire County
Brown, John	Berkeley County
Brown, Lemuel	Greenbrier County
Brown, Samuel	Greenbrier County
Brown, Thomas	Hampshire County
Brown, Timothy	Berkeley County
Brownfield, Robert	Monongalia County
Bryan, Christopher	Greenbrier County
Buchanan, William	Berkeley County
Buckhannon, William	Berkeley County
Buckles, James	Berkeley County
Buckles, Robert	Berkeley County
Buckles, William	Berkeley County
Buffington, David	Hampshire County
Buffington, Thomas	Hampshire County
Buffington, William	Hampshire County

Bull, John	Berkeley County
Bull, Robert	Berkeley County
Bull, William	Berkeley County
Bumgardner, Adam	Berkeley County
Bunnet, Samuel	Hampshire County
Burgess, Michael	Berkeley County
Burkett, Michael	Berkeley County
Burkham, Charles	Monongalia County
Burns, William	Berkeley County
Burr, Peter	Berkeley County
Burroughs, Booz	Monongalia County
Burroughs, Elijah	Monongalia County
Busard, Henry	Hampshire County
Butler, James	Greenbrier County
Butler, John	Berkeley County
Butler, John	Greenbrier County
Butler, Pearce	Berkeley County
Butler, Peter	Greenbrier County
Butt, John	Berkeley County
Byleton, Thomas	Berkeley County
Byrnside, James	Greenbrier County

CALDWELL, Andrew	Berkeley County
Caldwell, James	Berkeley County
Caldwell, James	Greenbrier County
Caldwell, John	Botetourt County
Caldwell, John	Monongalia County
Caldwell, William	Greenbrier County
Cambridge, Joseph	Monongalia County
Campbell, Duncan	Berkeley County
Campbell, *Captain* James	Berkeley County
Campbell, John	Hampshire County
Campbell, Robert	Berkeley County
Campbell, Thomas	Berkeley County
Campbell, William	Berkeley County
Canady, Thomas	Berkeley County
Cantley, John	Greenbrier County
Caperton, Adam	Greenbrier County
Caperton, Hugh	Greenbrier County
Car, James	Berkeley County
Carlile, David	Greenbrier County
Carlyle, William	Hampshire County
Carney, *Captain* James	Berkeley County
Carney, John	Berkeley County
Carney, William	Berkeley County
Carnover, Lyda	Berkeley County
Carnover, William	Berkeley County
Carpenter, Daniel	Monongalia County
Carpenter, Nicholas	Monongalia County
Carper, John	Berkeley County
Carr, Henry	Hampshire County
Carrell, Anthony	Monongalia County
Carroway, Thomas	Greenbrier County
Carson, James	Greenbrier County
Carter, Robert	Berkeley County
Cartright, Peter	Greenbrier County
Cartright, Peter	Monongalia County
Case, Michael	Monongalia County
Casey, Nicholas	Hampshire County
Casey, Peter	Hampshire County
Casey, Peter, *Junior*	Hampshire County
Cash, George	Berkeley County
Cassity, John	Monongalia County
Cassity, Peter, *Junior*	Monongalia County
Cassity, Peter, *Senior*	Monongalia County

19

Casteel, Joseph	Greenbrier County
Catly, Francis	Greenbrier County
Cavandish, William A.	Greenbrier County
Cavandish, W. H.	Greenbrier County
Ceever, Peter	Berkeley County
Chambers, James	Greenbrier County
Champion, James	Berkeley County
Champion, John	Berkeley County
Chenowith, John	Berkeley County
Chenowith, William	Berkeley County
Chesshire, Anne	Hampshire County
Chesshire, Joel	Hampshire County
Chick, George	Berkeley County
Childers, Rubin	Greenbrier County
Chinetts, Joseph	Berkeley County
Chinoworth, Isaac	Berkeley County
Chinoworth, Jonathan	Hampshire County
Chitan, John	Berkeley County
Chobe, Jacob	Hampshire County
Chrisman, Jacob	Hampshire County
Clark, Alexander	Greenbrier County
Clark, Walter	Berkeley County
Clarke, Walter	Berkeley County
Clawson, John	Berkeley County
Clay, Mitchell	Greenbrier County
Claycomb, Conrad	Berkeley County
Claycomb, Peter	Berkeley County
Claymo, Peter	Berkeley County
Claypole, Ephraim	Hampshire County
Claypole, James	Hampshire County
Claypole, John	Hampshire County
Clayton, Thomas	Hampshire County
Clegg, Alexander	Monongalia County
Clegg, William	Monongalia County
Clendinen, Adam	Greenbrier County
Clendinen, George	Greenbrier County
Clendinen, Robert	Greenbrier County
Clerk, Abraham	Hampshire County
Clever, Peter	Berkeley County
Cloak, George	Berkeley County
Close, Michael	Berkeley County
Close, Thomas	Monongalia County
Clutter, Jacob	Hampshire County

Cochran, James....................................Monongalia County
Cock, George....................................Berkeley County
Cockburn, Robert....................................Berkeley County
Coddy, David....................................Hampshire County
Coffenberger, Nicholas....................................Berkeley County
Coffenberry, George Lewis....................................Berkeley County
Coffenberry, Jacob....................................Berkeley County
Coffenberry, Lewis....................................Berkeley County
Coffenberry, Nicholas....................................Berkeley County
Coffman, Christian....................................Berkeley County
Coffman, Isaac....................................Berkeley County
Coffman, John....................................Berkeley County
Coldwell, Robert....................................Berkeley County
Colgan, Daniel....................................Berkeley County
Collet, Moses....................................Berkeley County
Collet, John....................................Berkeley County
Collett, Stephen....................................Berkeley County
Collins, Thomas....................................Hampshire County
Colvin, Stephen....................................Hampshire County
Cooke, Giles, *Junior*....................................Berkeley County
Cooke, Henry....................................Greenbrier County
Cooke, John....................................Greenbrier County
Cooke, Valentine....................................Greenbrier County
Cookus, Catherine....................................Berkeley County
Cookus, Henry....................................Berkeley County
Cookus, Michael....................................Berkeley County
Coon, Philip....................................Berkeley County
Coons, Jacob....................................Berkeley County
Coons, Philip....................................Berkeley County
Cooper, Abner....................................Greenbrier County
Cooper, Elizabeth....................................Berkeley County
Cooper, Leonard....................................Greenbrier County
Cooper, Simmon....................................Greenbrier County
Conkelenton, Jacob....................................Berkeley County
Conway, Cornelius....................................Berkeley County
Copenhever, Michael....................................Berkeley County
Core, Michael....................................Monongalia County
Cortney, Jacob....................................Berkeley County
Cotton, Benjamin....................................Greenbrier County
Cotton, Mary....................................Greenbrier County
Couden, James....................................Hampshire County
Coutsman, Benjamin....................................Berkeley County
Cowan, James....................................Berkeley County

Cowan, John	Berkeley County
Cowan, John, *Senior*	Berkeley County
Cowernove, Lydya	Berkeley County
Cowger, George	Hampshire County
Cowvenhover, Lidia	Berkeley County
Coyle, Joseph	Berkeley County
Cracroft, Thomas	Monongalia County
Craghead, Robert	Monongalia County
Craig, James	Berkeley County
Craig, John	Botetourt County
Craig, John	Hampshire County
Craig, William	Greenbrier County
Craightan, Robert	Berkeley County
Crain, James	Berkeley County
Crane, James	Berkeley County
Crane, John	Berkeley County
Crank, John	Berkeley County
Craughton, Robert	Berkeley County
Crawford, William	Botetourt County
Crawford, William	Greenbrier County
Crawford, William	Hampshire County
Crawford, *Colonel* William	Monongalia County
Creacraft, Samuel	Monongalia County
Creamer, Earnest	Berkeley County
Cred, Stophel	Berkeley County
Cremor, Aaron	Berkeley County
Cremor, George	Berkeley County
Crisap, *Colonel* Michael	Hampshire County
Crockett, *Colonel*	Berkeley County
Croll, David	Monongalia County
Cross, John	Berkeley County
Cross, William	Botetourt County
Cross, William	Monongalia County
Crouch, John	Monongalia County
Crouch, Joseph	Monongalia County
Crow, David	Hampshire County
Crow, Thomas	Berkeley County
Crumbly, William	Berkeley County
Cubberly, James	Hampshire County
Cunnard, James, *Junior*	Hampshire County
Cunnard, James, *Senior*	Hampshire County
Cunningham, Ann	Berkeley County
Cunningham, George	Berkeley County

Cunningham, *Captain* James............Hampshire County
Cunningham, Jesse...............Hampshire County
Cunningham, Patrick..............Berkeley County
Cunningham, Robert..............Hampshire County
Cunningham, William.............Hampshire County
Cunningham, William, *Junior*..........Hampshire County
Cunningham, William, *Senior*..........Hampshire County
Cuppy, John..................Hampshire County
Curle, Jeremiah................Hampshire County
Curry, William.................Botetourt County
Curtis, Job, *Junior*..............Berkeley County
Curtis, Job, *Senior*..............Berkeley County
Curviance, John................Monongalia County
Cutrack, John.................Hampshire County
Cutright, John.................Monongalia County

DAILEY, John	Berkeley County
Dalziel, James	Botetourt County
Dalziel, Thomas	Botetourt County
Daniel, Andrew	Berkeley County
Daniel, John	Berkeley County
Darke, William	Berkeley County
Darks, *Colonel*	Berkeley County
Darling, William	Hampshire County
Darlington, Meredith	Hampshire County
Darrat, Joseph	Monongalia County
Davenport, Abraham	Berkeley County
Davenport, Anthony	Berkeley County
Davenport, John	Berkeley County
Davenport, Stephen	Berkeley County
Davidson, George	Greenbrier County
Davidson, William	Botetourt County
Davidson, William	Greenbrier County
Davis, Edward	Berkeley County
Davis, John	Berkeley County
Davis, John	Greenbrier County
Davis, John	Monongalia County
Davis, Michael	Berkeley County
Davis, Patrick	Greenbrier County
Davis, Thomas	Hampshire County
Davis, Thomas	Monongalia County
Davis, William	Berkeley County
Davis, William	Greenbrier County
Davison, Daniel	Monongalia County
Dawkins, John	Berkeley County
Dawson, Isaac	Berkeley County
Dawson, Jacob	Berkeley County
Dawson, Thomas	Berkeley County
Day, John	Greenbrier County
Deaver, John	Hampshire County
Decker, John	Hampshire County
Dehart, Hannah	Botetourt County
Delaplane, John	Berkeley County
Delay, Henry	Monongalia County
Delong, Henry	Berkeley County
DeMose, James	Hampshire County
Demoss, Peter	Hampshire County
Demoss, Thomas	Hampshire County
Dennay, Simon	Monongalia County

Dent, John...Monongalia County
Devalt, Nicholas...Hampshire County
Dew, Samuel..Hampshire County
Dill, John...Berkeley County
Direly, Peter...Botetourt County
Dixon, John..Greenbrier County
Doak, John...Berkeley County
Dodridge, Joseph..Monongalia County
Doherty, Francis...Botetourt County
Donaly, Andrew...Greenbrier County
Doran, Peter...Hampshire County
Dorrough, Joseph..Monongalia County
Doster, Thomas..Berkeley County
Dougherty, William......................................Botetourt County
Downs, John...Berkeley County
Doyle, Edward...Botetourt County
Drandy, William...Greenbrier County
Duckwall, Frederick.....................................Berkeley County
Dudding, John...Botetourt County
Duke, John, *Senior*....................................Berkeley County
Dull, Christian...Hampshire County
Dull, Jacob..Hampshire County
Dullin, James..Greenbrier County
Dun, William..Berkeley County
Duncan, Mathew...Berkeley County
Dunlop, Moses...Botetourt County
Dunn, James...Monongalia County
Dunn, William...Greenbrier County
Durst, John..Berkeley County
Dustin, Richard..Berkeley County
Dustin, William..Berkeley County
Duvall, Cornelius..Berkeley County
Dyche, George...Berkeley County
Dyer, Charles..Greenbrier County

EAKINS, Thomas	Berkeley County
Eamaley, Henry	Berkeley County
Earson, Jacob	Hampshire County
Eason, Francis	Botetourt County
Eason, Samuel	Botetourt County
Eaton, Joseph	Berkeley County
Edgar, Thomas	Greenbrier County
Edmunds, Joan	Berkeley County
Edwards, Joseph	Berkeley County
Edwards, Thomas	Hampshire County
Ellis, Abraham	Berkeley County
Ellis, John	Berkeley County
Ellis, Joseph	Berkeley County
Ellis, Thomas	Greenbrier County
Ellison, James	Greenbrier County
Ellison, John	Greenbrier County
Ellison, Joseph	Greenbrier County
Emmery, Edwards	Hampshire County
Engle, John	Berkeley County
Ered, Stopael	Berkeley County
Ermentrout, Christopher	Hampshire County
Erry, George	Berkeley County
Estile, Bond	Greenbrier County
Estile, John	Greenbrier County
Estile, William	Greenbrier County
Estill, William	Greenbrier County
Etty, Henry	Berkeley County
Evans, David	Botetourt County
Evans, Elijah	Monongalia County
Evans, Isaac	Berkeley County
Evans, Isaac, *Junior*	Berkeley County
Evans, Isaac, *Senior*	Berkeley County
Evans, John	Berkeley County
Evans, John, *Junior*	Berkeley County
Evans, John	Hampshire County
Evans, John	Monongalia County
Evans, Joseph	Berkeley County
Evans, Peter	Botetourt County
Evans, Richard	Berkeley County
Evans, Thomas	Monongalia County
Everley, Casper	Monongalia County
Ewing, Baker	Botetourt County
Ewing, John	Berkeley County
Ewing, William	Greenbrier County

FAIRLY, Thomas..Hampshire County
Faries, David...Berkeley County
Faris, Robert...Berkeley County
Farler, Francis ....Greenbrier County
Farler, John..Greenbrier County
Farler, Thomas..Greenbrier County
Farlor, John..Greenbrier County
Fay, John...Berkeley County
Fayar, Alexander, *Senior*...............................Berkeley County
Fayter, Edward...Berkeley County
Feck, Andrew...Berkeley County
Fener, Vendle...Berkeley County
Fenner, Ninole..Berkeley County
Ferguson, Robert...Hampshire County
Ferguson, Thomas..Botetourt County
Ferrell, Robert..Monongalia County
Ferris, Arthur...Berkeley County
Ferris, David..Berkeley County
Ferris, William..Berkeley County
Fiddler, Edward...Hampshire County
Filson, Robert...Berkeley County
Fink, Harvey...Monongalia County
Fink, Henry..Monongalia County
Fisher, Adam..Hampshire County
Fisher, Isaac..Greenbrier County
Fisher, John...Berkeley County
Fitzpatrick, Charles......................................Berkeley County
Fitzpatrick, James..Greenbrier County
Fitzpatrick, John ....Greenbrier County
Fleece, Jacob..Berkeley County
Fleming, *Colonel* William..............................Botetourt County
Flin, George...Berkeley County
Fokner, Thomas...Berkeley County
Foreman, David...Hampshire County
Forman, Catherine..Hampshire County
Forman, Davis..Hampshire County
Forman, John, *Junior*...................................Hampshire County
Forman, Rueben..Berkeley County
Forman, *Captain* William..............................Hampshire County
Fost, Isaac...Berkeley County
Foster, Henry...Berkeley County
Foster, Isaac..Berkeley County
Foster, James...Berkeley County

Foster, John	Berkeley County
Fraisour, Ninole	Berkeley County
Franaway, Joseph	Berkeley County
Francisco, Lodowic	Botetourt County
Frank, George	Berkeley County
Frank, John	Berkeley County
Franklin, William	Botetourt County
Frayze, Joseph	Monongalia County
Frazer, David	Greenbrier County
Frazer, James	Greenbrier County
Frazer, John	Greenbrier County
Frazer, Martin	Greenbrier County
Freaney, Joseph	Berkeley County
French, George	Berkeley County
Freshour, Vendle	Berkeley County
Freys, Frederick	Berkeley County
Friend, Jonas	Monongalia County
Frise, Frederick	Berkeley County
Frits, Michal	Berkeley County
Frogg, William	Greenbrier County
Frost, William	Berkeley County
Frunch, John	Berkeley County
Fry, Henry	Hampshire County
Fry, Lodwick	Berkeley County
Fryatt, Botholomew	Berkeley County
Fryatt, John	Berkeley County
Fryer, Alexander	Berkeley County
Fuller, Joseph	Berkeley County
Fulton, David	Berkeley County

GACH, Jacob..Berkeley County
Gach, John..Berkeley County
Gaither, Ephraim.......................................Berkeley County
Galbreth, Hugh...Berkeley County
Galbreath, John..Berkeley County
Galloway, William......................................Botetourt County
Gambell, *Colonel*.....................................Greenbrier County
Gander, Gasper...Berkeley County
Gansway, Thomas, *Senior*..............................Berkeley County
Gant, John...Berkeley County
Gappan, Zachariah......................................Monongalia County
Garral, William..Berkeley County
Garrard, Jonnah..Monongalia County
Garrard, William.......................................Berkeley County
Garrett, William.......................................Berkeley County
Gasway, Thomas...Berkeley County
Gate, Jacob..Berkeley County
Gates, Horatio, *Major General*........................Berkeley County
Gates, Jacob...Berkeley County
Gatlif, Marthe...Greenbrier County
Gayts, Jacob...Berkeley County
Gelbraith, Elizabeth...................................Berkeley County
Gelder, Corper...Berkeley County
Gerard, David..Berkeley County
Gerrard, John..Berkeley County
Gibbony, Alexander.....................................Hampshire County
Gibson, Andrew...Berkeley County
Gibson, Hugh...Berkeley County
Gibson, Henry..Berkeley County
Gilkeson, James..Greenbrier County
Gill, James..Berkeley County
Gill, Robert...Berkeley County
Gill, Samuel...Botetourt County
Gillis, Thomas...Botetourt County
Gilmour, Sarah...Hampshire County
Gindell, Thomas..Monongalia County
Gist, Joseph...Berkeley County
Glaze, George..Hampshire County
Glen, John...Berkeley County
Glen, William..Berkeley County
Glove, John..Berkeley County
Goddart, John..Berkeley County
Goff, James..Monongalia County

33

Goff, Salathial	Monongalia County
Goodran, Thomas	Botetourt County
Goodson, Thomas	Botetourt County
Goosman, Abraham	Berkeley County
Gossett, Mathias	Berkeley County
Gossett, William	Berkeley County
Graham, Francis	Botetourt County
Graham, Jacob	Botetourt County
Graham, James	Greenbrier County
Graham, William	Greenbrier County
Grantam, John	Berkeley County
Grantam, Joseph	Berkeley County
Grantham, William	Berkeley County
Grattan, Thomas	Greenbrier County
Grave, John	Berkeley County
Gray, Hugh	Berkeley County
Gray, James	Botetourt County
Gray, John	Berkeley County
Gray, Jonathan	Berkeley County
Gray, William	Berkeley County
Grayson, Robert	Botetourt County
Green, Edward	Botetourt County
Green, Henry	Hampshire County
Green, James	Botetourt County
Green, William	Berkeley County
Greggs, Thomas	Berkeley County
Gregory, Andrew	Hampshire County
Griffin, Gordon	Greenbrier County
Griffith, John	Botetourt County
Griffith, John	Greenbrier County
Griffith, Thomas	Greenbrier County
Griffith, William	Greenbrier County
Griggor, George	Botetourt County
Griggs, Thomas	Berkeley County
Grooms, Abraham	Berkeley County
Grubb, William	Berkeley County
Grymes, Jonathan	Botetourt County
Guest, Joseph	Berkeley County
Guthrey, Francis	Botetourt County
Gwinn, Samuel	Greenbrier County
Gwinn, Thomas	Greenbrier County

HACALEY, Jacob	Berkeley County
Hackett, Nelson	Greenbrier County
Hadding, David	Monongalia County
Hageley, George	Berkeley County
Haggard, James	Greenbrier County
Hagle, John	Monongalia County
Hains, Catherine	Berkeley County
Hains, Michael	Berkeley County
Hains, Nathan	Berkeley County
Hair, James	Berkeley County
Hair, Jonas	Berkeley County
Hale, John	Botetourt County
Haley, Thomas	Berkeley County
Halkett, Thomas	Botetourt County
Hall, Alexander	Greenbrier County
Hall, Anthony	Berkeley County
Hall, Edward	Greenbrier County
Hall, George	Berkeley County
Hall, John	Berkeley County
Hall, Joseph	Berkeley County
Hall, Joseph	Hampshire County
Hall, Moses	Greenbrier County
Hall, Thomas	Berkeley County
Hall, William	Berkeley County
Halmark, George	Botetourt County
Hamersley, Robert	Berkeley County
Hamilton, Frederick	Berkeley County
Hamilton, James	Greenbrier County
Hamilton, Patrick	Monongalia County
Hamilton, *Captain* Thomas	Greenbrier County
Hammon, Phil	Greenbrier County
Hanckle, Barbara	Hampshire County
Hand, *General*	Berkeley County
Handley, Alexander	Botetourt County
Haney, Andrew	Botetourt County
Haney, George	Berkeley County
Haniker, Christian	Berkeley County
Hanna, Alexander	Botetourt County
Hanna, David	Greenbrier County
Hanna, Stephen	Berkeley County
Hannah, John	Berkeley County
Hannah, William	Berkeley County
Hannon, Mathew	Monongalia County

36

Hansaker, Christian	Berkeley County
Hansel, Michael	Berkeley County
Hanshaw, William	Berkeley County
Hanway, Samuel	Monongalia County
Haptonstall, Abraham	Greenbrier County
Hardin, *Evangelist*	Hampshire County
Hardin, Martin	Monongalia County
Hardin, *Major* John	Monongalia County
Hardy, John	Greenbrier County
Harlan, John	Berkeley County
Harland, Elonor	Berkeley County
Harlend, Elijah	Berkeley County
Harlin, Elias	Berkeley County
Harlin, Stephen	Berkeley County
Harman, George	Hampshire County
Harman, Nicholas	Berkeley County
Harmon, John	Greenbrier County
Harness, Adam	Hampshire County
Harness, George	Hampshire County
Harness, Jacob	Hampshire County
Harness, John	Hampshire County
Harness, John	Monongalia County
Harness, Michael	Hampshire County
Harper, John	Berkeley County
Harris, John	Hampshire County
Harris, Robert	Botetourt County
Harris, Samuel	Berkeley County
Harrison, Richard	Monongalia County
Harrison, Thomas	Monongalia County
Hart, George	Berkeley County
Hart, James	Berkeley County
Hart, John	Berkeley County
Hart, Thomas	Berkeley County
Hart, *Colonel* Thomas	Berkeley County
Hartly, Thomas	Berkeley County
Harvey, Robert	Botetourt County
Harvey, William	Botetourt County
Hase, John	Berkeley County
Hasell, Henry	Hampshire County
Haslep, Robert	Berkeley County
Hass, John	Berkeley County
Haun, Michael	Hampshire County
Hawk, Elijah	Berkeley County

Hawke, Andrew	Botetourt County
Hawkins, Joseph	Greenbrier County
Hay, Adam	Berkeley County
Hayly, Jacob	Berkeley County
Haymond, John	Monongalia County
Haynes, Nicholas	Botetourt County
Hays, John	Botetourt County
Hays, John, *Senior*	Berkeley County
Hays, Thomas	Berkeley County
Hays, William	Berkeley County
Hayzlet, Robert	Berkeley County
Hazle, Henry	Hampshire County
Heagle, John	Monongalia County
Heard, Edward	Berkeley County
Heath, Jonathan	Hampshire County
Heaton, Isaac	Hampshire County
Hedge, Joshua, *Senior*	Hampshire County
Hedge, Solomon	Hampshire County
Hedges, Benjamin	Hampshire County
Hedges, James	Hampshire County
Hedges, Jonas	Hampshire County
Hedges, Joseph	Hampshire County
Hedges, Samuel	Hampshire County
Heekman, Jacob	Hampshire County
Helm, Martin	Hampshire County
Henderson, Alexander	Botetourt County
Henderson, *Captain*	Greenbrier County
Henderson, David	Botetourt County
Henderson, James	Greenbrier County
Henderson, John	Botetourt County
Henderson, John	Greenbrier County
Henderson, Robert	Botetourt County
Henderson, Robert	Monongalia County
Hendricks, James	Berkeley County
Henry, Andrew	Botetourt County
Henry, John	Berkeley County
Hensil, Michael	Berkeley County
Henwood, William	Hampshire County
Herd, Edward	Berkeley County
Herling, Reese	Hampshire County
Hersecker, Christian	Berkeley County
Hesting, Reese	Hampshire County
Hevlick, Frederick	Berkeley County

Hider, Adam	Hampshire County
Hier, Leonard	Hampshire County
Hiett, Evan	Hampshire County
Higgenbottom, Moses	Greenbrier County
Higgins, John	Berkeley County
Higgins, John	Hampshire County
Higgins, Judith	Berkeley County
Higgins, Robert	Hampshire County
Highley, George	Monongalia County
Hill, Robert	Botetourt County
Hill, Samuel	Botetourt County
Hinton, John	Monongalia County
Hird, Edward	Berkeley County
Hite, *Colonel* Abraham	Hampshire County
Hite, Francis	Berkeley County
Hite, Gasper	Hampshire County
Hite, Joseph	Berkeley County
Hite, *Colonel* Thomas	Berkeley County
Hizer, John	Berkeley County
Hoff, Cornelious	Hampshire County
Hoff, Lawrence	Hampshire County
Hoff, Philip	Botetourt County
Hoff, Sarah	Hampshire County
Hoffman, John	Hampshire County
Hogdon, Jeremiah	Botetourt County
Hogg, Aaron	Hampshire County
Holdar, Thomas	Monongalia County
Holladay, James	Berkeley County
Hollis, Bur	Berkeley County
Holoback, Thomas	Hampshire County
Holstine, Henry	Botetourt County
Hopkins, James	Berkeley County
Hord, John	Monongalia County
Horn, Frederick	Berkeley County
Horn, George	Berkeley County
Hornback, James	Hampshire County
Hornback, Mary	Hampshire County
Hornback, Michael	Hampshire County
Hornback, *Captain* Samuel	Hampshire County
Houghman, Christopher	Hampshire County
House, William	Hampshire County
Housman, David	Berkeley County
Housman, Martin	Berkeley County

Hought, Peter................................Monongalia County
Hout, George................................Berkeley County
Houtts, Paul................................Berkeley County
Hover, Mathias................................Berkeley County
Howard, John................................Botetourt County
Howard, Martin................................Berkeley County
Howell, David................................Botetourt County
Howell, Joshua................................Botetourt County
Howman, Sithman................................Hampshire County
Huckleberry, Joseph................................Monongalia County
Hudson, William................................Monongalia County
Huff, Benjamin................................Botetourt County
Huff, Philip................................Botetourt County
Huffman, Christopher................................Hampshire County
Huffman, George................................Berkeley County
Huffman, Peter................................Berkeley County
Huggard, James................................Greenbrier County
Huggard, James, *Junior*................................Greenbrier County
Huggard, William................................Greenbrier County
Hulse, Elizabeth................................Berkeley County
Humphries, John................................Greenbrier County
Humphries, Richard................................Greenbrier County
Humphries, Uriah................................Botetourt County
Hungate, John................................Botetourt County
Hunter, Henry................................Greenbrier County
Hurt, George................................Berkeley County
Hust, Henry................................Berkeley County
Hustan, James................................Greenbrier County
Huston, John................................Monongalia County
Hutchison, George................................Botetourt County
Hutchison, James................................Botetourt County
Hutchison, John................................Greenbrier County
Hutchison, Samuel................................Greenbrier County
Hutchison, William................................Botetourt County
Hutchison, William................................Greenbrier County
Hutton, *Captain*................................Hampshire County
Hutton, Isaac................................Hampshire County
Hutton, John................................Berkeley County
Hutton, *Colonel* Moses................................Hampshire County

INGLE, Philip..Berkeley County
Inskeep, Abraham..Hampshire County
Isbel, George..Berkeley County

JACK, James..Berkeley County
Jackson, George..Monongalia County
Jackson, John..Monongalia County
Jackson, *Captain* Robert..Berkeley County
James, John..Berkeley County
Jamison, John..Greenbrier County
Jaques, Denton..Berkeley County
Jarritt, David..Greenbrier County
Jarritt, James..Greenbrier County
Jarritt, Jesse..Greenbrier County
Jarritt, Owen..Greenbrier County
Jenkin, Jonathan..Hampshire County
Jenkins, Bartholomew..Monongalia County
Jenkins, George..Berkeley County
Jenkins, Evan..Hampshire County
Jenkins, Jacob..Hampshire County
Jenkins, Martha..Monongalia County
Jennings, William..Hampshire County
Job, Thomas..Berkeley County
John, *Lieutenant* Lemuel..Monongalia County
John, Robert..Berkeley County
John, Samuel..Berkeley County
John, William..Monongalia County
Johnson, Abraham..Hampshire County
Johnson, Adam..Hampshire County
Johnson, Eve..Botetourt County
Johnson, John..Botetourt County
Johnson, John..Hampshire County
Johnson, Michael..Hampshire County
Johnson, Michael..Monongalia County
Johnson, Okey..Hampshire County
Johnson, William..Berkeley County
Johnson, William..Botetourt County
Johnson, William..Greenbrier County
Johnson, William..Hampshire County
Johnston, Arwalker..Greenbrier County
Johnston, James..Greenbrier County
Johnston, William..Greenbr er County
Jones, Isaac..Hampshire County
Jones, John..Greenbrier County
Jones, Sam..Berkeley County
Jones, William..Hampshire County

43

KANADY, Thomas	Hampshire County
Karns, Michael	Monongalia County
Kavanaugh Charles	Greenbrier County
Kay, John	Berkeley County
Kay, John	Hampshire County
Kearsley, John	Berkeley County
Kebber, George	Berkeley County
Keeney, David	Greenbrier County
Keeny, Michael	Greenbrier County
Kehore, David	Greenbrier County
Kelley, William	Berkeley County
Kelly, John	Greenbrier County
Kelly, Michael	Greenbrier County
Kenady, Daniel	Berkeley County
Kenady, Robert	Berkeley County
Kenedy, John	Berkeley County
Kenedy, Robert	Berkeley County
Kenedy, Samuel	Berkeley County
Kenedy, Thomas	Berkeley County
Kenny, John	Berkeley County
Kenny, Thomas	Greenbrier County
Kent, Joseph	Hampshire County
Ker, James	Berkeley County
Keran, Patrick	Hampshire County
Kerney, John	Berkeley County
Kerney, Peter	Berkeley County
Kershman, Martin	Berkeley County
Keyes, Humphrey	Berkeley County
Keys, John	Berkeley County
Kidner, George	Hampshire County
Killian, Phenihas	Monongalia County
Kilpatrick, Roger	Greenbrier County
Kimberlane, Pauler	Botetourt County
Kimberline, Jacob	Hampshire County
Kimble, John	Hampshire County
Kincaid, Thomas	Greenbrier County
King, Charles M.	Berkeley County
King, Robert	Botetourt County
Kint, Jesse	Hampshire County
Kirk, *Lieutenant*	Greenbrier County
Kirk, Joseph	Berkeley County
Kisckor, John	Berkeley County
Kiser, Martin	Berkeley County

Kiser, Martin..Greenbrier County
Kisenger, Matthias.....................................Greenbrier County
Kisinger, Andrew.......................................Greenbrier County
Kitchen, James..Greenbrier County
Kittle, Jacob...Monongalia County
Knotts, Banjamin..Monongalia County
Kolton, Thomas..Greenbrier County
Korbin, Joseph...Berkeley County
Kuykendall, Abraham....................................Hampshire County
Kuykendall, Henry.......................................Hampshire County
Kuykendall, Katherine...................................Hampshire County
Kyle, Joseph...Berkeley County
Kyle, Joseph...Botetourt County
Kyle, William..Botetourt County
Kysor, Martin..Greenbrier County

LACEY, James..Greenbrier County
Lacey, Mark..Greenbrier County
Lacey, William..Greenbrier County
Lacey, William, *Junior*..............................Greenbrier County
Laferty, William...Greenbrier County
Lafferty, Thomas..Berkeley County
Laidley, Thomas...Monongalia County
Lander, Henry...Hampshire County
Lane, Thomas..Berkeley County
Lansisco, Henry..Hampshire County
Lapsly, John..Botetourt County
Largent, James..Hampshire County
Largent, John..Hampshire County
Largent, William...Hampshire County
Larkin, Hugh..Berkeley County
Larue, John...Hampshire County
Lauderdale, James.......................................Botetourt County
Lauderdale, John...Botetourt County
Lauferty, William..Greenbrier County
Lawrence, Michael.......................................Hampshire County
Lawson, Thomas..Berkeley County
Laymon, Joseph...Botetourt County
Leatherdale, James......................................Botetourt County
Lee, Charles..Berkeley County
Lee, James..Berkeley County
Lee, *Doctor* John......................................Berkeley County
Lee, Lancelott...Berkeley County
Lemmen, Robert..Berkeley County
Lemmen, William...Berkeley County
Lemon, Alexander..Berkeley County
Lemon, William...Berkeley County
Lewis, Andrew...Botetourt County
Lewis, George...Berkeley County
Lewis, Thomas..Botetourt County
Lewis, William..Greenbrier County
Light, Peter..Berkeley County
Lilborn, Mary...Berkeley County
Lilly, David..Hampshire County
Linch, Charles..Hampshire County
Linder, Jacob, *Senior*...............................Berkeley County
Linder, Lawrence...Berkeley County
Linsay, Samuel...Botetourt County
Little, Daniel...Berkeley County

Little, James...Monongalia County
Little, William..Berkeley County
Littlejohn, John...Berkeley County
Littlejohn, William...Berkeley County
Lloyd, James...Botetourt County
Loague, Samuel..Botetourt County
Lock, George..Berkeley County
Lock, Jacob..Berkeley County
Lock, Jacob..Hampshire County
Lock, John..Berkeley County
Lock, William...Berkeley County
Lockhart, *Captain* Pat...................................Botetourt County
Lockridge, John...Greenbrier County
Logan, James..Berkeley County
Logan, John..Botetourt County
Long, *Captain*...Berkeley County
Long, Jacob..Hampshire County
Looney, Absolom...Botetourt County
Looney, Joseph...Botetourt County
Lower, George...Hampshire County
Lowery, James..Berkeley County
Lucas, *Captain* Edward..................................Berkeley County
Lucas, William..Berkeley County
Lyle, Hugh...Berkeley County
Lyle, John...Berkeley County
Lyle, Robert...Berkeley County
Lynch, *Captain* Charles.................................Hampshire County
Lynch, Patrick...Hampshire County
Lyon, Michael...Hampshire County
Lysle, Hugh, *Senior*.....................................Berkeley County
Lytle, David..Botetourt County

McAFEE, James	Botetourt County
McAfee, James	Greenbrier County
McBride, James	Hampshire County
McBride, John	Hampshire County
McCalister, James	Berkeley County
McCalister, James, *Junior*	Berkeley County
McCane, James	Botetourt County
McCarrel, John	Berkeley County
McCarty, Edward	Hampshire County
McCarty, Thomas	Hampshire County
M'Caull, Robert	Berkeley County
M'Cinney, John	Berkeley County
McClanahan, David	Botetourt County
McClanahan, Samuel	Botetourt County
McClanahan, *Captain* William	Botetourt County
McClellen, William	Botetourt County
McClung, Charles	Greenbrier County
McClung, Samuel	Greenbrier County
McClure, Malcom	Botetourt County
McClure, Nathaniel	Botetourt County
McClure, Samuel	Botetourt County
McConnall, Abraham	Berkeley County
McConnel, William	Berkeley County
McCormack, Edward	Berkeley County
McCormick, Andrew	Berkeley County
McCormick, James	Berkeley County
McCormick, John	Berkeley County
McCoy, Joseph	Berkeley County
McCullough, Alexander	Berkeley County
McCullough, Joseph	Berkeley County
McCullock, William	Berkeley County
McDonald, Alexander	Botetourt County
McDonald, Andrew	Berkeley County
McDonald, Edward	Botetourt County
McDonald, John	Botetourt County
McDonald, Mrs. Mary	Botetourt County
McDonald, Susanna	Botetourt County
McDowell, George	Botetourt County
McElheny, Robert	Botetourt County
McElheney, Samuel	Botetourt County
McFadden, Charles	Botetourt County
McFarland, John	Monongalia County
McFarran, Andrew	Greenbrier County

McFerran, Martin............................Botetourt County
McFerran, Samuel...........................Botetourt County
McFerran, Thomas...........................Botetourt County
McGarrah, Samuel..........................Greenbrier County
McGeorge, Thomas..........................Botetourt County
McGill, *Major* Charles....................Hampshire County
McGovan, James.............................Berkeley County
McHatten, Alexander........................Berkeley County
McHeron, Samuel............................Berkeley County
McIntire, David.............................Berkeley County
McIntire, Nicholas..........................Berkeley County
McIntire, Thomas...........................Berkeley County
McIntosh, *General*.........................Hampshire County
McKever, Paul..............................Hampshire County
McKewen, Robert...........................Berkeley County
McKewn, Michael...........................Berkeley County
McKey, Alexander..........................Greenbrier County
McKienan, Peter............................Berkeley County
McKinney, Andrew..........................Berkeley County
McKnight, Charles..........................Berkeley County
McKnight, *Reverend* John..................Berkeley County
McKnight, Robert...........................Berkeley County
McLean, John...............................Berkeley County
McMahon, John.............................Monongalia County
McMakin, Thomas...........................Botetourt County
McMurry, Thomas...........................Botetourt County
McMurry, Thomas...........................Greenbrier County
McMurry, William..........................Botetourt County
McNeal, Daniel.............................Hampshire County
McNeely, David............................Botetourt County
McNeely, William..........................Botetourt County
McNeil, John...............................Hampshire County
McNeile, John..............................Greenbrier County
McNutt, James.............................Greenbrier County
McPheron, Samuel..........................Berkeley County
McPherson, Daniel..........................Berkeley County
McRoberts, Samuel.........................Botetourt County

MACE, Nicholas............................Hampshire County
Maclin, William............................Monongalia County
Madcalf, Allen.............................Berkeley County
Madcalf, Vechel............................Berkeley County
Maden, Patrick............................Berkeley County

52

Madison, John	Botetourt County
Madison, Thomas	Botetourt County
Madison, William	Botetourt County
Maedin, Patrick	Berkeley County
Magby, Mathew	Berkeley County
Magill, *Major* Charles	Hampshire County
Magill, Robert	Berkeley County
Manford, William	Berkeley County
Mann, Adam	Greenbrier County
Mann, Jacob	Greenbrier County
Mann, Moses	Botetourt County
Marchel, James	Berkeley County
Mares, Stephen	Berkeley County
Markes, William	Greenbrier County
Marks, John	Berkeley County
Marks, Samuel	Berkeley County
Marlet, Abraham	Berkeley County
Marrin, Barnet	Greenbrier County
Marrs, Stephen	Hampshire County
Marrs, Henry Munday	Berkeley County
Marsh, Henry	Hampshire County
Martin, Agnes	Botetourt County
Martin, *Colonel* Charles	Monongalia County
Martin, George	Monongalia County
Martin, John	Hampshire County
Martin, Jonathan	Botetourt County
Martin, *Captain* Joshua	Botetourt County
Martin, Margaret	Berkeley County
Martin, Peter	Berkeley County
Martin, Thomas	Berkeley County
Martin, Thomas	Botetourt County
Martin, Valentine	Botetourt County
Martin, William	Botetourt County
Mason, Edward	Berkeley County
Mason, James	Berkeley County
Mason, James	Botetourt County
Mason, William	Botetourt County
Mason, William	Greenbrier County
Massey, Jacob	Greenbrier County
Mathews, Archer	Greenbrier County
Mawzer, Adam	Hampshire County
Maxwell, *Captain* Alexander	Monongalia County
May, Agnes	Botetourt County

May, David	Botetourt County
May, Jacob	Hampshire County
Mays, Stephen	Botetourt County
Maze, Richard	Botetourt County
Melatt, Abraham	Berkeley County
Melvin, John	Berkeley County
Melvin, Joseph	Berkeley County
Melvin, Thomas	Berkeley County
Mercer, John	Berkeley County
Mercer, Robert	Berkeley County
Michal, Micheli	Berkeley County
Mickie, James	Greenbrier County
Mickie, William	Greenbrier County
Middleton, Thomas	Berkeley County
Mifford, Jacob	Botetourt County
Milburn, William	Hampshire County
Miles, George	Berkeley County
Miles, John	Berkeley County
Miles, Richard	Berkeley County
Miller, *Lieutenant* Anthony	Hampshire County
Miller, Charles	Greenbrier County
Miller, Christian	Berkeley County
Miller, Conrad	Berkeley County
Miller, David	Berkeley County
Miller, David	Greenbrier County
Miller, Henry	Berkeley County
Miller, Hugh	Berkeley County
Miller, Hugh	Greenbrier County
Miller, Isaac	Hampshire County
Miller, Jacob	Greenbrier County
Miller, Jacob	Hampshire County
Miller, James	Berkeley County
Miller, John	Berkeley County
Miller, John	Greenbrier County
Miller, John	Hampshire County
Miller, Martin	Berkeley County
Miller, Michael	Hampshire County
Miller, Philip	Berkeley County
Miller, Robert	Berkeley County
Miller, Thomas	Botetourt County
Miller, Zacariah	Berkeley County
Milliken, John	Berkeley County
Mills, Hugh	Botetourt County

Mills, James	Botetourt County
Mills, John	Botetourt County
Mills, Mary	Botetourt County
Mills, Thomas	Monongalia County
Mineer, David	Monongalia County
Minnis, Robert	Monongalia County
Mitchell, David	Botetourt County
Mitchell, James	Botetourt County
Mitchell, *Captain* Joseph	Berkeley County
Mitchell, Robert	Greenbrier County
Moler, Adam	Berkeley County
Moone, Jacob	Berkeley County
Moor, Benjamin	Berkeley County
Moor, John	Berkeley County
Moor, Robert	Berkeley County
Moore, Anthony	Hampshire County
Moore, James	Botetourt County
Moore, John	Botetourt County
Moore, Joseph	Berkeley County
Moore, Michael	Monongalia County
More, Cato	Berkeley County
More, Jacob	Berkeley County
More, Robert	Berkeley County
Morefield, Samuel	Monongalia County
Morgan, Abel	Berkeley County
Morgan, Abraham	Berkeley County
Morgan, David	Monongalia County
Morgan, Jane	Berkeley County
Morgan, John	Hampshire County
Morgan, M.	Hampshire County
Morgan, Morgan	Berkeley County
Morgan, Morgan	Monongalia County
Morgan, Richard	Berkeley County
Morgan, William	Berkeley County
Morgan, *Major* William	Berkeley County
Morgan, Zackquill	Monongalia County
Morris, John	Greenbrier County
Morris, Joseph	Monongalia County
Morris, Leonard	Greenbrier County
Morris, Robert	Berkeley County
Morris, William	Greenbrier County
Morrison, James	Berkeley County
Morrow, Charles	Berkeley County

Mours, John......Hampshire County
Mozor, Adam......Hampshire County
Muldrough, Hugh......Botetourt County
Mulliner, Nat......Berkeley County
Munford, William......Berkeley County
Murphy, James......Hampshire County
Murphy, John......Berkeley County
Murphy, Valentine......Berkeley County
Murphy, William......Berkeley County
Murray, Zack......Berkeley County
Muse, George......Hampshire County
Mussin, Jean......Botetourt County
Myers, Mary......Berkeley County
Myers, Peter......Berkeley County
Myles, George......Berkeley County
Myre, John......Berkeley County

NAFFSINGER, John	Berkeley County
Neale, William	Hampshire County
Neason, Richard	Hampshire County
Neely, Andrew	Botetourt County
Neely, James	Botetourt County
Neely, James, *Junior*	Botetourt County
Neely, James, *Senior*	Botetourt County
Neely, John	Botetourt County
Neely, William	Botetourt County
Neff, Henry	Monongalia County
Nelson, Charles	Monongalia County
Nevill, Joseph	Hampshire County
New, Peter	Monongalia County
Newlan, James	Berkeley County
Newkirk, Jonas	Berkeley County
Nicholas, John	Greenbrier County
Nicholas, Thomas	Greenbrier County
Nixon, George	Hampshire County
Noble, Anthony	Berkeley County
Noble, John	Berkeley County
Noos, Jacob	Monongalia County
Norris, George	Hampshire County
Norse, James	Berkeley County
Nours, James	Berkeley County
Nowland, Thomas	Berkeley County
Nowlin, John	Berkeley County

OAR, James	Berkeley County
Obanion, Joseph	Hampshire County
O'Bannon, Joseph	Hampshire County
O'Bryan, Adam	Monongalia County
Obryon, Adam	Monongalia County
Ocheltree, Michael	Botetourt County
Ocletree, James	Botetourt County
Odear, James	Greenbrier County
Ogdon, Joseph	Berkeley County
Ogle, Harmlas	Botetourt County
Oldham, Samuel	Berkeley County
Olive, Joseph	Berkeley County
Orenduff, Henry	Berkeley County
Orr, James	Berkeley County
Orr, John	Berkeley County
Orr, William	Berkeley County
Orrich, Nicholas	Berkeley County
Osborn, Jeremiah	Hampshire County
Osbourn, David	Berkeley County
Osbourn, William	Berkeley County
Osburn, George	Hampshire County
Osburn, James	Berkeley County
Otan, John	Greenbrier County
Oug, Isaac	Berkeley County
Ove, James	Berkeley County
Ove, John	Berkeley County
Owens, William	Monongalia County
Owin, Thomas	Berkeley County
Ozburn, Jesse	Greenbrier County
Ozburn, John	Botetourt County

PAIN, Thomas	Berkeley County
Painter, George	Berkeley County
Painter, Jacob	Berkeley County
Parish, Edward	Monongalia County
Park, Samuel	Greenbrier County
Parker, Benjamin	Hampshire County
Parker, George	Hampshire County
Parker, Nathaniel	Hampshire County
Parker, Robert	Hampshire County
Parker, William	Berkeley County
Parkes, George	Greenbrier County
Parks, John	Berkeley County
Parks, Samuel	Hampshire County
Parsinger, Christopher	Botetourt County
Parsinger, Jacob	Botetourt County
Parsons, James	Greenbrier County
Parsons, James	Hampshire County
Parsons, Thomas	Hampshire County
Paterson, James	Greenbrier County
Patterson, George	Botetourt County
Patterson, William	Berkeley County
Paul, Andy	Botetourt County
Paul, John	Berkeley County
Pauling, Henry	Botetourt County
Pearsall, John	Hampshire County
Peck, John	Botetourt County
Pedan, John	Botetourt County
Piersall, John	Hampshire County
Pendleton, J.	Monongalia County
Pendleton, *Colonel* John	Greenbrier County
Pendleton, Philip	Berkeley County
Pentecost, *Colonel* Dorsey	Monongalia County
Persons, Thomas	Hampshire County
Peterson, John	Berkeley County
Petijohn, Moleston	Greenbrier County
Pettey, Ebenzer	Monongalia County
Petty, John William, *Junior*	Monongalia County
Petty, John William, *Senior*	Monongalia County
Petro, Henry	Monongalia County
Phillips, Thomas	Berkeley County
Phillips, Thomas	Monongalia County
Philson, Robert, *Junior*	Berkeley County
Philson, Robert, *Senior*	Berkeley County

Pierce, Andrew..Berkeley County
Pierey, James...Botetourt County
Pightet, Frederick..Botetourt County
Piles, David...Monongalia County
Piles, Zackariah..Monongalia County
Pindell, Thomas..Monongalia County
Pinkerton, Robert...Berkeley County
Piper, John...Greenbrier County
Pisel, Peter..Berkeley County
Pittser, Mathew...Berkeley County
Pittser, Michael..Berkeley County
Pitzer, John..Botetourt County
Pitzer, Mathias...Berkeley County
Pitzer, Michael...Berkeley County
Poage, George...Botetourt County
Poague, Robert..Botetourt County
Poland, Cornelius...Berkeley County
Porter, William...Hampshire County
Porterfield, Alexander....................................Berkeley County
Porterfield, George.......................................Berkeley County
Porterfield, William......................................Berkeley County
Poston, Elias...Hampshire County
Powell, William...Hampshire County
Power, Felty..Hampshire County
Power, Martin...Hampshire County
Power, Valentine..Hampshire County
Prather, Jeremiah...Berkeley County
Preston, Thomas...Botetourt County
Preston, William..Botetourt County
Pricket, Jacob..Monongalia County
Pricket, Joseph...Monongalia County
Prior, Joseph...Botetourt County
Province, Sarah...Monongalia County
Prunty, John..Hampshire County
Pryor, John...Botetourt County
Pryor, Luke...Botetourt County
Pugh, Daniel..Hampshire County
Pugh, Robert..Hampshire County
Pusey, James..Botetourt County
Putman, Peter...Hampshire County
Pyzle, Peter..Berkeley County

QUALEY, Patrick..Berkeley County
Quick, Tunis...Berkeley County
Quigley, James...Berkeley County

RADELIFF, John.................................Monongalia County
Rainy, John...Berkeley County
Ralston, Mathew................................Botetourt County
Ramsey, Charles.................................Monongalia County
Ramsey, John......................................Monongalia County
Randall, Abel......................................Hampshire County
Randall, Jacob....................................Hampshire County
Raney, John..Berkeley County
Rankin, Benjamin..............................Berkeley County
Rannels, William................................Hampshire County
Ransom, Richard................................Berkeley County
Ratcliffe, Edward...............................Hampshire County
Raulston, John....................................Greenbrier County
Rayburn, John.....................................Botetourt County
Read, George.......................................Hampshire County
Reads, *Captain*................................Berkeley County
Ready, William....................................Berkeley County
Reasoner, Garret.................................Hampshire County
Reasoner, Jacob..................................Hampshire County
Reburn, George...................................Greenbrier County
Redick, Joseph....................................Berkeley County
Reddock, Joseph.................................Berkeley County
Reece, David.......................................Botetourt County
Reece, John..Berkeley County
Reed, George.......................................Hampshire County
Reed, John..Berkeley County
Reed, John..Hampshire County
Regar, Burhil.......................................Berkeley County
Reid, John..Berkeley County
Reid, Thomas......................................Botetourt County
Ren, Nickholas....................................Berkeley County
Rennick, John......................................Hampshire County
Rennick, *Mr*. Rt...............................Greenbrier County
Rennick, William................................Hampshire County
Rennicks, William..............................Greenbrier County
Reynolds, George................................Berkeley County
Reynolds, John....................................Botetourt County
Rheny, Michael...................................Greenbrier County
Rhim, John...Berkeley County
Rhods, Jacob.......................................Berkeley County
Rice, Nicholas.....................................Berkeley County
Richards, Christian............................Botetourt County
Richards, Christopher........................Botetourt County

Richards, Joshua..Berkeley County
Richardson, Aaron...Monongalia County
Richardson, Daniel...Hampshire County
Richardson, Joseph..Botetourt County
Rickert, Peter...Berkeley County
Ridgeway, John...Berkeley County
Ridgeway, Philip...Berkeley County
Ried, Alexander..Greenbrier County
Riffle, Elenor..Monongalia County
Riley, George...Berkeley County
Riley, John..Berkeley County
Rippe, Mathew..Berkeley County
Rippy, Mathew..Berkeley County
Ritchie, William..Botetourt County
Roark, John...Greenbrier County
Robenson, Alexander.......................................Berkeley County
Robenson, James...Berkeley County
Roberts, Daniel...Berkeley County
Roberts, Sam..Berkeley County
Roberts, Thomas...Berkeley County
Roberts, William...Berkeley County
Robertson, James..Berkeley County
Robey, Prior...Hampshire County
Robey, William...Hampshire County
Robinett, Jesse..Botetourt County
Robinson, James..Botetourt County
Robinson, John..Botetourt County
Robinson, Joseph...Botetourt County
Robinson, William...Botetourt County
Robinson, William...Monongalia County
Rodgers, John...Greenbrier County
Rodgers, Lewis..Monongalia County
Rogers, Alexander...Berkeley County
Rogers, Leonard..Berkeley County
Rogers, William..Hampshire County
Rollings, Aron..Berkeley County
Ronamus, Andrew..Berkeley County
Ronan, Gatron..Monongalia County
Roots, George...Berkeley County
Roper, Nicholas...Berkeley County
Rorebaugh, John...Hampshire County
Rose, Jonathan...Berkeley County
Ross, John...Botetourt County

St CLAIR, *Mr.*	Greenbrier County
Salt, Edd	Berkeley County
Sarackwell, Samuel	Berkeley County
Sargent, Richard	Berkeley County
Savage, John	Hampshire County
Scaggs, James	Greenbrier County
Scaggs, John	Greenbrier County
Scandlan, Robert	Botetourt County
Schoolcraft, Austeen	Monongalia County
Schoolcraft, Matthias	Monongalia County
Schriekock, Leonard	Berkeley County
Scott, Charles	Botetourt County
Scott, David	Monongalia County
Scott, *Major* George	Berkeley County
Scott, Jacob	Monongalia County
Scott, James	Botetourt County
Scott, James	Monongalia County
Scott, Thomas	Monongalia County
Scott, William	Botetourt County
Scott, William	Greenbrier County
Sea, George	Greenbrier County
Sea, John	Greenbrier County
Sea, Michael	Greenbrier County
Seaman, Jonah	Berkeley County
Seamon, Jonathan	Berkeley County
See, George	Hampshire County
See, Michael	Hampshire County
Sefer, John	Berkeley County
Sergen, Richard	Berkeley County
Server, Gasper	Botetourt County
Server, John	Botetourt County
Sever, Peter	Berkeley County
Sewel, David	Berkeley County
Sewel, John	Berkeley County
Sewel, Timothy	Berkeley County
Seymour, Felix	Hampshire County
Seymour, Richard	Hampshire County
Seymour, Thomas	Hampshire County
Seyster, Daniel	Berkeley County
Shack, Andrew	Berkeley County
Shad, George	Hampshire County
Shankes, William	Greenbrier County
Shanklin, Robert	Hampshire County

Sharkey, James	Botetourt County
Sharkey, Nicholas	Botetourt County
Sharkey, Patrick	Botetourt County
Sharp, Andrew	Berkeley County
Sharp, Thomas	Berkeley County
Sharr, Martin	Berkeley County
Shaver, Boston	Botetourt County
Shaver, Michael	Berkeley County
Sheep, John	Berkeley County
Sheetz, Philip	Berkeley County
Shepherd, Abraham	Berkeley County
Shepherd, John	Berkeley County
Shepherd, John	Greenbrier County
Shepherd, Thomas	Berkeley County
Shepherd, William	Berkeley County
Sherer, Andrew	Berkeley County
Sherer, Archibald	Berkeley County
Sherer, Henry	Berkeley County
Sheriff, John	Berkeley County
Sherley, Robert	Berkeley County
Sherly, James	Berkeley County
Sherly, Jonas	Berkeley County
Shields, John	Berkeley County
Shields, William	Berkeley County
Shirley, Jerve	Berkeley County
Shirley, Walter	Berkeley County
Shirly, John	Berkeley County
Shively, John	Berkeley County
Shivers, Catherine	Hampshire County
Shobe, Leonard	Hampshire County
Shobe, Martin	Hampshire County
Shobe, Rudolph	Hampshire County
Shock, Andrew	Berkeley County
Shoemaker, John	Greenbrier County
Shoemaker, Peter	Greenbrier County
Sholl, Nicholas	Hampshire County
Sholton, Thomas	Greenbrier County
Shriver, Peter	Berkeley County
Shrowle, John	Botetourt County
Siling, Andrew	Berkeley County
Simpson, Alexander	Botetourt County
Simpson, Alexander	Hampshire County
Simpson, Jeremiah	Monongalia County

Simpson, William .... Monongalia County
Simson, John .... Hampshire County
Simson, Jonathan .... Hampshire County
Sisson, George .... Greenbrier County
Skidmore, James .... Botetourt County
Skillern, George .... Botetourt County
Slaughter, Smith .... Berkeley County
Slaughter, William .... Berkeley County
Small, Adam .... Berkeley County
Smallwood, George .... Berkeley County
Smiley, Walter .... Botetourt County
Smith, Alexander .... Berkeley County
Smith, Charles .... Botetourt County
Smith, David .... Botetourt County
Smith, *Captain* Francis .... Botetourt County
Smith, Frederick .... Botetourt County
Smith, George .... Botetourt County
Smith, Granville .... Botetourt County
Smith, Henry .... Monongalia County
Smith, James .... Botetourt County
Smith, James .... Greenbrier County
Smith, James .... Hampshire County
Smith, John .... Berkeley County
Smith, Jonathan .... Monongalia County
Smith, Michael .... Botetourt County
Smith, Nicholas .... Monongalia County
Smith, Solomon .... Berkeley County
Smith, William .... Berkeley County
Smith, William .... Monongalia County
Smyth, A. .... Botetourt County
Smyther, George .... Monongalia County
Snickers, Edward .... Berkeley County
Snider, George .... Monongalia County
Snider, Jacob .... Berkeley County
Snither, George .... Monongalia County
Snodgrass, Isaac .... Botetourt County
Snodgrass, James .... Botetourt County
Snodgrass, John .... Berkeley County
Snodgrass, John, *Junior* .... Berkeley County
Snodgrass, Joseph .... Botetourt County
Snodgrass, Robert .... Berkeley County
Snodgrass, William .... Botetourt County
Snyder, John .... Monongalia County

Sommers, Michael..Berkeley County
Sommerville, Joseph.......................................Berkeley County
Southwood, Edward?.......................................Berkeley County
Springer, Edward...Botetourt County
Springer, Zadock..Monongalia County
Springstone, Elizabeth....................................Monongalia County
Sprouls, John..Botetourt County
Stalmaker, Felty..Monongalia County
Stalmaker, Jacob...Monongalia County
Stanby, Isaac..Berkeley County
Stapleton, Charles..Botetourt County
Stapleton, William...Botetourt County
Starkey, Frederick..Hampshire County
Starling, James..Monongalia County
Statts, Joseph...Monongalia County
Steel, Robert...Botetourt County
Stephen, *General* Adam.................................Berkeley County
Stephens, Richard..Berkeley County
Stephens, Robert...Berkeley County
Stephenson, Andrew.......................................Botetourt County
Stephenson, Ann..Berkeley County
Stephenson, James...Hampshire County
Stepp, Martin...Berkeley County
Sterling, John...Botetourt County
Stevens, Edmund...Botetourt County
Stewart, Charles..Botetourt County
Stewart, John...Botetourt County
Stewart, Robert...Berkeley County
Stockton, George...Berkeley County
Stockton, George...Monongalia County
Stokes, John...Hampshire County
Stookey, Abraham..Hampshire County
Storm, Jacob...Berkeley County
Strader, Christopher.......................................Hampshire County
Strader, Philip..Berkeley County
Straitone, Jacob...Monongalia County
Strawther, William...Berkeley County
Strode, James..Berkeley County
Strode, Jeremiah..Berkeley County
Strode, John...Berkeley County
Stroop, Henry..Berkeley County
Strother, Benjamin...Berkeley County
Stroud, James...Berkeley County

Stroud, James	Greenbrier County
Strydor, Philip	Berkeley County
Stuart, James	Hampshire County
Stuart, John	Greenbrier County
Stuart, Walter	Botetourt County
Stubbs, William	Berkeley County
Stump, George	Hampshire County
Stump, Leonard	Hampshire County
Stump, Michael	Hampshire County
Summer, Hezekiah	Botetourt County
Summer, John Ludowick	Berkeley County
Sutton, Benjamin	Monongalia County
Swearingen, Benoni	Berkeley County
Swearingen, *Mrs.* Hannah	Berkeley County
Swearingen, Hezekiah	Berkeley County
Swearingen, John, *Senior*	Monongalia County
Swearingen, *Captain* Josiah	Berkeley County
Swearingen, Van	Berkeley County
Swearingen, *Colonel* Van	Berkeley County
Swift, Godwin	Berkeley County
Swim, Lazarus	Berkeley County
Swim, Mathias, *Junior*	Berkeley County
Swim, Mathias, *Senior*	Berkeley County
Swingly, Peter	Berkeley County
Switzer, Henry	Botetourt County
Switzer, Valentine	Hampshire County
Swobe, John	Greenbrier County
Swope, Michael	Monongalia County
Sylers, Jacob	Berkeley County
Systor, Daniel	Berkeley County

TABB, Elizabeth ....Berkeley County
Tabb, George ....Berkeley County
Tabler, Adam ....Berkeley County
Tabler, George ....Berkeley County
Tailor, John ....Berkeley County
Tailor, Samuel ....Berkeley County
Talbert, William ....Berkeley County
Talbot, William ....Berkeley County
Tapp, John ....Hampshire County
Tarance, Archibald ....Berkeley County
Tate, Magnus ....Berkeley County
Taws, Andrew ....Berkeley County
Taylor, Edward ....Berkeley County
Taylor, Isaac ....Botetourt County
Taylor, Jonathan ....Botetourt County
Taylor, Simon ....Hampshire County
Tays, Andrew ....Berkeley County
Taze, Thomas ....Greenbrier County
Teesenholer, John ....Berkeley County
Terry, Jasper ....Botetourt County
Terry, William ....Botetourt County
Thomas, Evan ....Hampshire County
Thomas, Ezekial ....Hampshire County
Thomas, James ....Hampshire County
Thomas, Richard ....Botetourt County
Thomas, William ....Monongalia County
Thompson, Cornelius ....Berkeley County
Thompson, David ....Hampshire County
Thompson, James ....Greenbrier County
Thompson, John ....Greenbrier County
Thompson, John ....Hampshire County
Thompson, Robert ....Greenbrier County
Thompson, William ....Botetourt County
Thornberry, Benjamin ....Berkeley County
Thornberry, Thomas ....Berkeley County
Thornberry, William ....Berkeley County
Throckmorton, Lewis ....Hampshire County
Throckmorton, Robert ....Berkeley County
Tichenal, Moses ....Hampshire County
Tilderoy, Andrew ....Berkeley County
Timmonds, Samuel ....Hampshire County
Timmons, Bryan ....Berkeley County
Tipton, Sylvester ....Hampshire County

76

Titus, Joseph	Botetourt County
Tivault, Nicholas	Hampshire County
Tivebaugh, Daniel	Hampshire County
Tomelson, Charles	Monongalia County
Tomlison, Joseph	Hampshire County
Tool, John	Berkeley County
Tooley, Charles	Botetourt County
Tosh, Jonathan	Botetourt County
Traviss, Robert	Hampshire County
Tray, Simon	Monongalia County
Trenor, Michael	Monongalia County
Trig, John	Berkeley County
Trotter, James	Greenbrier County
Troy, John	Monongalia County
Turman, Ignatius	Botetourt County
Turman, James	Botetourt County
Turner, John	Berkeley County
Turner, Joseph	Berkeley County
Turner, Thomas	Berkeley County
Turner, William	Hampshire County
Tusenholer, John	Berkeley County
Tyler, Henry	Hampshire County
Tylor, Isaac	Greenbrier County

VANBIBBER, John..Greenbrier County
Vanbibber, Peter..Greenbrier County
Vance, *Reverend* Hugh....................................Berkeley County
Vance, Robert..Berkeley County
Vancelheller, John..Berkeley County
Vandivender, Cornelius....................................Hampshire County
VanLear, John..Botetourt County
Vanmeter, Abraham..Berkeley County
Vanmeter, Abraham..Hampshire County
Vanmeter, Abraham, *Junior*..............................Berkeley County
Vanmeter, Abraham, *Senior*..............................Berkeley County
Vanmeter, Garret..Hampshire County
Vanmeter, Henry..Hampshire County
Vanmeter, Isaac...Berkeley County
Vanmeter, Isaac...Hampshire County
Vanmeter, *Captain* Jacob..................................Hampshire County
Vanmeter, Jacob..Berkeley County
Vanmeter, John..Berkeley County
Vanmeter, John, *Senior*...................................Berkeley County
Vanmeter, *Major* John.....................................Berkeley County
Vanmeter, *Captain* Joseph................................Hampshire County
Vanmeter, Solomon...Hampshire County
Vanpelt, Tune...Berkeley County
Vansant, Josiah...Botetourt County
Vanse, William..Hampshire County
Vanswearingen..Berkeley County
Vanswearingen, *Colonel*..................................Berkeley County
Vardier, James..Berkeley County
Vaught, Casper..Botetourt County
Veaill, Thomas..Botetourt County
Vencenholer, John..Berkeley County
Vestervelt, James...Berkeley County
Vilet, Thomas...Berkeley County
Viney, John...Greenbrier County
Vineyard, Christian...Botetourt County
Violet, Thomas..Berkeley County
Volgomote, David...Berkeley County
Vostall, William...Berkeley County

WADDLE, James	Berkeley County
Walker, Henry	Botetourt County
Walker, William	Botetourt County
Wallace, Caleb	Botetourt County
Waller, John	Berkeley County
Wallingsford, Benjamin	Berkeley County
Wallingsford, Joseph	Berkeley County
Walter, John	Berkeley County
Ward, Isaac	Berkeley County
Ward, Joseph	Berkeley County
Ward, Joseph	Botetourt County
Ward, Sylvester	Hampshire County
Ward, W.	Botetourt County
Ward, W.	Greenbrier County
Ward, William	Botetourt County
Warden, William	Hampshire County
Ware, James	Berkeley County
Warman, Francis	Monongalia County
Warren, James	Berkeley County
Warwick, John	Monongalia County
Washington, *Colonel* John Aug.	Berkeley County
Washington, Samuel	Berkeley County
Washington, William Augustine	Berkeley County
Watkins, John	Botetourt County
Watkins, Philip	Botetourt County
Watson, John	Berkeley County
Watson, Samuel	Berkeley County
Watterson, Henry	Botetourt County
Watts, *Doctor* Peter	Berkeley County
Wattwood, George	Botetourt County
Wease, Michael	Hampshire County
Weatherington, Samuel	Botetourt County
Weaver, Christopher	Berkeley County
Webb, John	Monongalia County
Webb, William	Botetourt County
Wedner, George	Berkeley County
Weigle, George	Berkeley County
Welch, Alexander	Greenbrier County
Wells, William	Botetourt County
Welsh, Michael	Berkeley County
Welsh, Robert	Berkeley County
Welton, Davis	Hampshire County
Welton, Jesse	Hampshire County

Welton, Job..Hampshire County
Welton, John...Hampshire County
Welton, *Captain* William.............................Hampshire County
West, Benjamin..Botetourt County
West, John..Berkeley County
Westfall, Abraham..Hampshire County
Westfall, George...Monongalia County
Westfall, Jacob...Monongalia County
Westfall, John...Hampshire County
Westfall, William..Monongalia County
Wever, George..Hampshire County
Whealey, George..Greenbrier County
White, John...Berkeley County
White, Thomas..Berkeley County
Whiting, Henry...Berkeley County
Whiting, Mathew...Berkeley County
Whitman, Matthias..Monongalia County
Whitten, Matthew..Berkeley County
Wiagle, George...Berkeley County
Wigle, Philip...Berkeley County
Wile, Frederick...Berkeley County
Wilkeson, John..Monongalia County
Willett, James...Berkeley County
William, John...Monongalia County
Williams, J. ....Monongalia County
Williams, James..Greenbrier County
Williams, Jerome...Berkeley County
Williams, Joseph...Greenbrier County
Williams, Richard..Hampshire County
Williams, Thomas..Botetourt County
Williams, Thomas..Greenbrier County
Williams, Vincent..Hampshire County
Williamson, Jacob...Berkeley County
Williamson, John...Hampshire County
Williamson, Peter, *Junior*...........................Berkeley County
Williamson, William.......................................Berkeley County
Willis, *Captain* Francis...............................Berkeley County
Willis, Richard Francis...................................Berkeley County
Willis, Robert Carter.....................................Berkeley County
Wills, William..Botetourt County
Willson, Andrew..Botetourt County
Willson, David...Botetourt County
Willson, Jacob...Berkeley County

Willson, James	Monongalia County
Willson, Mathew	Botetourt County
Willson, Thomas	Botetourt County
Wilson, Andrew	Botetourt County
Wilson, Andrew	Greenbrier County
Wilson, Benjamin	Monongalia County
Wilson, David	Hampshire County
Wilson, Davis	Hampshire County
Wilson, Edward	Berkeley County
Wilson, Elinor	Botetourt County
Wilson, Hugh	Berkeley County
Wilson, James	Berkeley County
Wilson, James	Greenbrier County
Wilson, John	Berkeley County
Wilson, John	Hampshire County
Wilson, Mary	Berkeley County
Wilson, Samuel	Berkeley County
Wilson, William	Berkeley County
Wilson, William	Hampshire County
Wilson, William	Monongalia County
Wincoop, Adrian	Berkeley County
Windsor, Jonathan	Greenbrier County
Winning, James	Berkeley County
Wisehart, Christopher	Berkeley County
Wisenburg, George	Berkeley County
Withers, John	Botetourt County
Withers, William	Berkeley County
Wodrow, Andrew	Hampshire County
Wolford, Martin	Berkeley County
Wood, Davis	Hampshire County
Woodfin, Nicholas	Greenbrier County
Woodfin, Samuel	Greenbrier County
Woodfin, Thomas	Greenbrier County
Woods, Adam	Greenbrier County
Woods, Andrew	Botetourt County
Woods, Andrew	Greenbrier County
Woods, Archibald	Botetourt County
Woods, Archibald	Greenbrier County
Woods, John	Botetourt County
Woods, John	Greenbrier County
Woods, Michael	Greenbrier County
Woods, Peter	Greenbrier County
Woods, Susannah	Greenbrier County

Woods, Thomas..Botetourt County
Woods, Thomas..Greenbrier County
Woods, William..Greenbrier County
Wooley, David..Botetourt County
Wooley, William..Botetourt County
Woolf, Elizabeth..Berkeley County
Woolford, Martin..Berkeley County
Wootts, *Doctor* Peter..Berkeley County
Worley, Brace..Monongalia County
Worley, Caleb..Botetourt County
Worley, Michael..Hampshire County
Wormley, Ralph..Berkeley County
Worthington, Ephriam..Berkeley County
Worthington, Margaret..Berkeley County
Wright, George..Berkeley County
Wright, James..Botetourt County
Wright, Peter..Botetourt County
Wright, Thomas..Greenbrier County
Wright, William..Berkeley County
Wyle, Frederick..Berkeley County

YANCY, John ....Botetourt County
Yates, Peter ....Hampshire County
Yeater, Peter ....Hampshire County
Yeats, Andrew ....Berkeley County
Yoakham, Conrad ....Greenbrier County
Yoakman, George ....Monongalia County
Yoakum, George ....Hampshire County
Yoakum, Philip ....Hampshire County
Yocum, Elizabeth ....Hampshire County
Yolkiom, George ....Greenbrier County
York, Ezekial ....Monongalia County
Young, Edward ....Botetourt County
Young, Nicholas ....Berkeley County

EXCERPTS FROM REVOLUTIONARY WARRANTS

The selections which follow are taken from the old records of Berkeley, Botetourt, Greenbrier, Hampshire, and Monongalia: counties of Virginia during the time of the Revolutionary war, but now included in the state of West Virginia, where they represent forty-two of the fifty-five counties in that state.

Printed forms for warrants were provided, but the commissioner serving the warrants often found his supply exhausted and wrote on any bit of paper that came to hand. Sometimes warrants are found written on a leaf torn from an old account book, the items of the account left on the other side.

The excerpts given are the merest hint of the vast amount of interesting information found in the Virginia Revolutionary Public Claims and Tax Books.

Differences in spelling and change in the meanings of ordinary English words since the Revolutionary period and today give these old records other attractions than the purely historical.

"**William Brady** is allowed Two Pounds Ten Shillings for the ferrage of wagons and Teams in the Service of the State which is ordered to be certified."

Berkeley County Warrant

"**Colonel Thomas Hart** produced in Court Certificate for two Waggons and Teams impressed for the use of the State in the Continental Service which being approved of is ordered to be certified."

Berkeley County Warrant

"**William Wright** produced in Court a Certificate for a Horse impressed for the use of the State in the Continental Service valued at forty-five pounds, about fourteen hands three inches high, four years old which valution is approved and of which is ordered to be certified."

Berkeley County Warrant

"**Adam Stephen** assignee of **John Vanmeter Senr.** is allowed Thirty One Pounds Twelve Shillings and five Pence for five head of Beef Cattle furnished the State which is ordered to be certified."

Berkeley County Warrant

"**Walter Clark** produced in Court a Certificate for a Horse impressed for the use of the State in the Continental Service valued at forty-five pounds, but the said Clark produced in Court Sufficient Testimony that the Horse was worth more. It is the opinion of the Court that he be allowed fifty pounds, he is at least fifteen hands high six years old which is ordered to be certified."

Berkeley County Warrant

"**Benjamin Rankin** is allowed nine pounds seven shillings and six pence for Horse Hire for seventy-five days for the use of the State which is ordered to be certified."

Berkeley County Warrant

"To **William Johnson** for riding express four days."

Greenbrier County Warrant

"To **William Arbuckle** for Hand Cuffs for a Deserter."

Greenbrier County Warrant

"To **Thomas Edgar** for his service as Commissary for the County."

Greenbrier County Warrant

"To **Patrick Davis** for nineteen pounds of butter."

Greenbrier County Warrant

"To **James Huggard** for six diets."

Greenbrier County Warrant

"To **Sam Brown** for Dieting express twelve days and attendance when sick."

Greenbrier County Warrant

"To **John Rodgers** for one blanket."

Greenbrier County Warrant

"Order that the sum of twenty pounds be allowed **William H. Cavendish** for two years services as Commissioner for the Specific Tax in the year 1780 and 1781."

Greenbrier County Warrant

"**David Morgan** for repairing guns allowed the amount of the amount by the Court."

Monongalia County Warrant

"Ordered that the sum of Ten Pounds be allowed **William Arbuckle** for his services as Commissioner for the Specific Tax for the year 1780."

Greenbrier County Warrant

"The same allowance made to **George Davidson** for the same service in 1781."

Greenbrier County Warrant

"Twelve pounds is allowed **William Estill** for the same service for the years 1780 and 1781."

Greenbrier County Warrant

"Six pounds is allowed **George Clendenen** for the same service in the year 1780."

Greenbrier County Warrant

"Eight pounds **William Cavendish** for laying the county into districts and collecting Cloaths and Beeves."

Greenbrier County Warrant

"Ordered that **Christopher Bryan** be allowed seven pounds ten shillings for a horse furnished **Captain Henderson's** company of Militia on their march to Point Pleasant which horse was lost."

Greenbrier County Warrant

"Order that a Note given by **Colonel William Crawford** to **Colonel Charles Martin** be settled agreeable to the scale of depreciation."

Monongalia County Warrant

The depreciation referred to in the above warrant is strikingly illustrated in the warrants of John Higgins and Colonel Van Swearingen. John Higgins received twenty-four shillings per pound for beef on the hoof and Colonel Van Swearingen received six hundred and thirty pounds for thirty-one and one-half bushels of wheat.

"Received for Public use of **John Higgins** Seven Head of Grass Cattle estimated Two Thousand three Hundred Weight Neat Beef for which payment at the rate of Twenty Four Shillings per pound shall be made according to the assurance contained in the Resolution of the Assembly of November 15, 1780."

Hampshire County Warrant

"Received from **Colonel Van Swearingen** Thirty One and One Half Bushels of wheat for the Use and Account of the State of Virginia for which the said Colonel Van Swearingen is entitled to receive from the Treasury of the said State the sum of Six Hundred and Thirty Pounds current Money, agreeable to an Act of Assembly."

Berkeley County Warrant

"To **George Stockton** for eight diets for men was produced and allowed by the Court on the State at nine pence per diet."

Monongalia County Warrant

"To **Francis Warman** for three days packing with three horses allowed by the Court two shillings six pence per day for each horse and two shillings six pence per day for driver."

Monongalia County Warrant

"To **David Piles** for ninety pounds of Bear meat and forty pounds venison allowed by the Court for the bear meat 3 pence per pound and 1 and one half pence per pound for the venison."

Monongalia County Warrant

"**Henry Fink** produced a certificate from **Captain Alexander Maxwell** for 240 pounds Pork taken by said Maxwell for public use which voucher the court has passed and valued at 30 shillings per hundred."

Monongalia County Warrant

"To **Zacquil Morgan** for sundry amounts amounting to 191 pounds no shillings no pence."

Monongalia County Warrant

"**James Dunn** produced a receipt for 90 rations 'allowed by the Court one shilling and six pence per ration on the State."

Monongalia County Warrant

"Received from **William Green** six Bushels of Wheat for the Use and on Account of the State of Virginia for which the said William Green is entitled to receive from the Treasury of the said State the Sum of one hundred and Twenty Pounds current Money agreeable to an act of Assembly entitled 'An Act for procuring a Supply of Provisions and other Necessaries for the Use of the Army.' "

Berkeley County Warrant

"There is due **Philip Ingle, Henry Stroop, William Lucas, Michael Hensil** and **Andrew Shock** the sum of twenty-one hundred pounds for thirty Bushels of Wheat furnished by the said Philip Ingle, etc., for the use of the State of Virginia."

Berkeley County Warrant

John Campbell's Apple Claim

The public claim of John Campbell of Hampshire County for damages for apples destroyed by "Three Brigades of Pack Horses" quartered in his meadow is the only one of its kind in the West Virginia index.

We the Subscribers at the request of Mr. John Campbell being duly qualified before William Buffington Gentleman Justice of the said County have inquired by the Testimony of two Credible Witnesses into Damage done the said John Campbell by Three Brigades of Pack Horses turned into the said John Campbells Meadow by William Thompson, Thomas Lewis and Michael Gleowe, Horse Masters transporting Provisions from the Western Parts of Virginia to Fort Pitt for the use of the Expedition carrying on under general McIntosh are of opinion that the said John Campbell hath sustained Damage by the said Horses destroying a Quantity of Apples and a Hogshead filled with some of them under the same enclosure with the Meadow which the said Horse Masters engaged to Guard to the value of Ten Pounds. Given under our Hand this 6th Day of October, 1778.

(Signed) Samuel Dew
(Signed) Isaac Parsons

I hereby certify that the within names Samuel Dew and Isaac Parsons being Credible Housekeepers in my Neighborhood were duly qualified for the Purpose within mentioned as also the two Witnesses before me this 6th Day of October, 1778.

(Signed) William Buffington

Hampshire County September Court 1783. The within Claim was offered to the Court by John Campbell which (I kno no Law admits of its being Allowed and certified in the Common Way) they were of Opinion he ought to be allowed Forty Shillings for the within Damages.

(Signed) Test Andrew Wodrow, Clerk.

In the Virginia Revolutionary Public Claims the letters M.D. after a name are as apt to be an abbreviation of mule-driver as an abbreviation of doctor of medicine; the word "doctor" or "surgeon" being usually written to distinguish members of the medical profession.

The office of Justice was important in Revolutionary times and all Justices were entitled to the use of the word "Gentleman" after their signatures.

Diet, in these old warrants refers to board as "to Sam Brown for Dieting Express ten days." Express meant "riders of express", just as commissary often referred to the person who issued or received supplies.

Many persons have Virginia Revolutionary ancestors whose service to the cause was non-military. The record of this service is almost sure to be found in the archives of the Virginia State Library, which has the largest manuscript collection in the United States with the single exception of the Library of Congress. But the material is unindexed and the writing often very difficult to read, making a long and tedious search necessary. This booklet is the first attempt to list these public claims, and it is the intention of the author to index the public claims of the Revolutionary period for every county in Virginia. Half of the counties have been completed and it is hoped that the other half will be indexed by the end of the year.